Cupids and Cherubs

Cupids and Cherubs

DIVINE INSPIRATIONS
IN CRAFT AND DECORATING

LOUISE OWENS & KATE TULLY

Photography by Quentin Bacon

Contents

Contents

Divine inspirations

This is a book of inspirations as much as a book of instructions. Certainly, there are full instructions for making twenty projects — all of them items of beauty, individuality and style.

And, aware that few of us have the luxury of unlimited spare time, we have collected together a range of projects that are planted firmly in the 'minimum effort, maximum effect' category. You'll notice that none of the projects needs a dozen 'how to' photographs to explain how it is made.

While — as you will discover — these projects combine to produce high impact room settings and truly charming gift ideas, you will be delighted when you see that each one of them is within the capabilities of us all, even those of us who don't regard ourselves as accomplished craftspeople.

But more than just a collection of projects, there are so many gorgeous photographs to savour, plus suggestions and encouragement to go beyond what is described in these pages and to apply the ideas, techniques and patterns to anything your imagination can evoke.

The greatest enjoyment in undertaking craft and decorating projects is surely the creation of something that is entirely 'you'. All of us take our inspirations from some source or other, and our intention in producing this book is to provide you with a bountiful source.

The projects described are an excellent starting point and will help you to learn new techniques and polish up on skills you have already. We hope you will then start to say to yourself: 'What else could I do with this?', and to experiment with new applications to devise something that is really 'you'.

Divine inspirations

In the list of materials which accompanies each project, we have described in general terms the materials required. To find out exactly which paint colours we used, check the 'What we used' box at the end of the project.

However, don't let these lists deter you from using appropriate materials you may have in your craft drawers already, or from using our lists as a guideline only and varying the materials to suit your own taste.

We have chosen the theme of cupids and cherubs because ... well, they are simply very hard to resist! While most of us are familiar (through a barrage of reproduction papers, cards and other items) with the cherubs popularised in Victorian arts and crafts, the cherub is of course much older than late nineteenth century. In our projects we have generally avoided Victorian representations of cherubs with their often too sweet faces and colouring, and have worked instead with both older and more contemporary cherub motifs.

We think you will enjoy this new look at some of history's favourite offspring.

Look, imagine, create and enjoy!

Louise Owens
and Kate Tully

Heavenly Hosts

PROJECTS FOR
THE TABLE AND GARDEN

Embellished decoupage serving dish

Stippled garden wall statue

Verdigris and dappled gold pots

Verdigris and dappled gold lamp

Sharon
Elizabeth
Therasa

Sharon
Elizabeth

Heavenly Hosts

Dine in exalted company with our cherub-inspired projects for an outdoor buffet and table setting. Antiqued gold charms are threaded on gold cord to ring plant pots and a lamp-shade, while cherubs also ring our decoupage dish embellished with gold paint. The plant pots and lamp have been given a combination of two striking paint treatments — verdigris and dappled gold — to create a sense of aged elegance. This feeling is reinforced by the stippled cherub statue, who has the appearance of having looked down over many heavenly repasts.

LEFT

Continue your heavenly hosts theme with some cherubic finishing touches. These ready-made placecards featuring a cherub motif have been inscribed using the calligraphy instructions and alphabet on pages 82–85. Tie napkins with a generous bow and tuck a cherub into the knot. Photographed at The Parterre Garden, Sydney.

Embellished Decoupage

SERVING DISH

MATERIALS

Purchased dish (glass or other) with smooth upper surface

Acrylic undercoat and binder

Antique green background paint

Artist's acrylics in pearl, warm white and gold

Sea sponge

Gift wrap featuring cherubs

Curved nail scissors

Craft glues (e.g. Aquadhere and Clag)

Paint brush

Workable fixative spray (from craft suppliers)

Tack cloth (from craft suppliers)

Clear sealer

800 and 1200 wet-and-dry sandpaper

Varnish brush

Varnish

Mineral turps

1 Apply undercoat and binder: glass may need up to five coats for a smooth, stable surface.

2 Apply three coats of background paint in antique green.

3 Using the sponge and the artist's acrylics, apply a cloud-like effect. You can include more of the background paint, too, in this effect. You may like to practise on paper first. Add a line of gold around the rim of the dish.

4 Spray front and back of gift wrap with workable fixative; this helps hold the paper together and makes it easier to handle. When dry, cut out suitable cherubs using nail scissors.

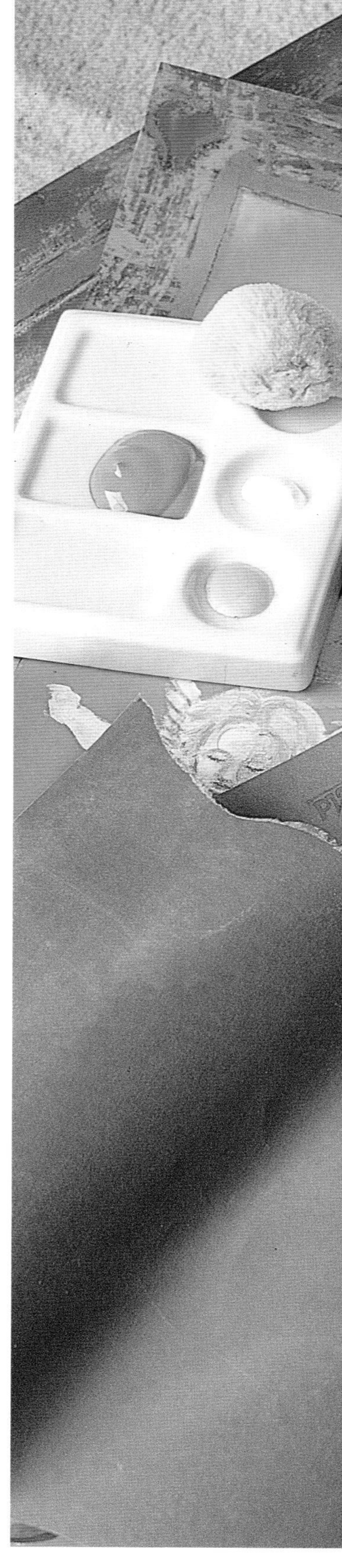

RIGHT

After painting the cloud-like effect onto the dish, arrange the cut-out cherubs until you are happy with their placement.

continued on page 15

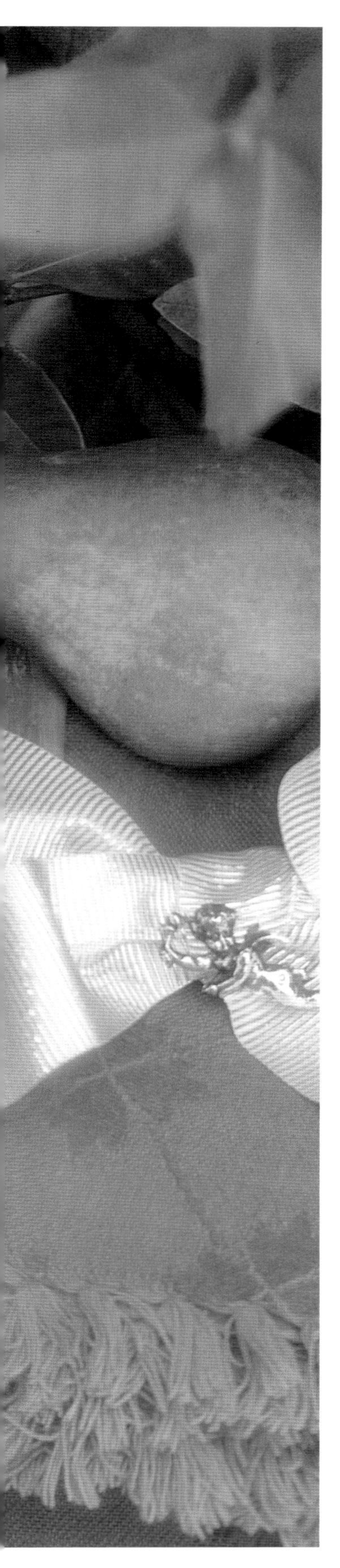

5 Arrange cherubs around the dish. When you are happy with the arrangement, glue them to the dish. Use a wet sponge to remove any air bubbles, so that the images lie perfectly flat against the dish.

6 When the glue is dry, embellish the tips of the cherubs' wings with gold, and other features with other suitable colours if you wish. Sponge on a little more of the background colour to help blend in the figures.

7 Leave to dry for at least two days, then seal with clear sealer.

8 When the sealer is dry, you can start varnishing the dish. First wipe the dish with the tack cloth to remove all dust, then apply an even coat of varnish. Continue applying varnish once a day until you have built up the required number of coats. Between coats, suspend varnish brush in a jar of mineral turps.

Apply 10 coats of varnish, then sand carefully in one direction only, using 800 wet-and-dry sandpaper. Apply three more coats, then sand with 1200 wet-and-dry sandpaper. Apply two final coats. The back of the dish does not require the same number of coats — three is sufficient.

WHAT WE USED

Paints are Matisse Antique Green Background Paint and Jo Sonja acrylics in Smoked Pearl, Warm White and Rich Gold. Gift wrap is 'Cherubs and Ribbons' (DLW40) and 'Cherubs and Clouds' (DLW39) from Gallery Collection.

Serving dish by Alexandra Gray

Stippling

GARDEN WALL STATUE

MATERIALS

Artist's acrylics in turquoise blue, turquoise green, raw umber, white, antique white and yellow

Purchased statue

25 mm stippling brush

WHAT WE USED

Paints are Jo Sonja Artist Gouache in Pthalo Blue, Pthalo Green, Raw Umber, White; Matisse Antique White; Chromacryl Cool Yellow.

1 Mix first four colours to desired basecoat colour. Dip stippling brush into paint, dab lightly onto paper a few times then apply to statue with a quick dabbing motion. Allow to dry at least 30 minutes.

2 Add antique white and yellow to make a greener tone for shading. Stipple this colour into the contours of the statue to help define detail.

ABOVE
The statue will have two coats of paint: an all-over basecoat and a darker coat in the contours only, for shading.

RIGHT
Garden wall statue by Samantha Small

Painted Finishes

VERDIGRIS AND DAPPLED GOLD POTS

MATERIALS

Terracotta plant pots
Sealer
25mm brush
Artist's acrylics in pale gold, turquoise blue, turquoise green, raw umber, black, white, antique white and yellow
Soft cotton cloth
Methylated spirits
Varnish
Sea sponge
Gold size
Gold leaf
Cotton gloves
8 gold charms for each pot
Fine gold cord to go around rim of each pot
Craft glue

1 Apply sealer to outside of pots.

2 Mix raw umber, black and white to create a copper colour for basecoat, and apply two coats to the part of the pot below the rim, brushing on in vertical strokes. Leave to dry at least 30 minutes.

3 Mix turquoise blue, turquoise green, raw umber and white to create a sea blue colour, then apply one coat, again in even, vertical strokes. Leave to dry at least 30 minutes.

4 Mix colours as for second coat plus antique white and yellow to create the final green colour, and apply one coat in the same manner. Leave to dry at least one hour.

5 Dip cloth into methylated spirits and gently rub patches of the painted surface, using vertical strokes only. Rub until you are just back to the basecoat (copper colour); the second coat (blue colour) will also be revealed.

TOP RIGHT
With a cloth dipped in methylated spirits, gently rub off patches of the painted surface until you get back to the copper-coloured first coat.

FAR RIGHT
Verdigris and dappled gold pots by Samantha Small

continued on page 20

RIGHT

Once the verdigris finish is complete, start on the rim by applying a generous coat of pale gold.

FAR RIGHT

Add raw umber over the pale gold, then you are ready to apply small pieces of gold leaf to complete the dappled effect. You can buy both oil-based and acrylic gold size. The oil-based size takes longer to dry and therefore gives you more time to work with it, but is slightly messier to clean up.

WHAT WE USED

Bondcrete sealer. Paints are Jo Sonja Artist Gouache in Pthalo Blue, Pthalo Green, Raw Umber, Black, White and Pale Gold; Matisse Antique White; Chromacryl Cool Yellow. Winsor & Newton Gold Size

6 When you have achieved the effect you like, apply varnish over the whole of the painted surface.

7 Brush on one generous coat of pale gold all around rim of pot. Don't worry about brush marks — these only add to the effect. Leave to dry at least 30 minutes.

8 Mix raw umber with water to a light creamy consistency. Using sea sponge, apply over pale gold base. Apply a little at a time, building up darker and lighter areas. Leave to dry at least 30 minutes.

9 Dab gold size randomly over rim. Leave to cure for approximately 10 minutes.

10 Wearing cotton gloves, gently break gold leaf into small pieces and press over the size. Check the overall effect, and apply more size and leaf if you wish. When the size is completely dry, gently rub off any excess leaf with your fingers.

You might like to practise these finishes on another surface (such as smooth scrap timber) before applying it to your pots.

For instructions on adding the gold charms, see page 22.

VERDIGRIS AND DAPPLED GOLD LAMP

MATERIALS

Purchased lamp base and shade

Sealer

25 mm brush

Artist's acrylics in pale gold, turquoise blue, turquoise green, raw umber, black, white, antique white and yellow

Soft cotton cloth

Methylated spirits

Varnish

Sea sponge

Gold size

Gold leaf

Cotton gloves

10 gold charms

Fine gold cord to go around rim of shade

Adhesive tape

Craft glue

1 Follow instructions on pages 18–20 for painted finishes. Apply verdigris finish to body of lamp base and dappled gold finish to base and top.

2 Measure a length of fine gold cord sufficient to go around rim of lamp shade plus 5cm. Before cutting, bind ends tightly with adhesive tape to prevent fraying. Cut cord and thread through holes at back of charms.

3 Space charms evenly along length of cord, then stick cord and charms to shade using craft glue. Finish off ends neatly at back of shade, underneath a charm.

WHAT WE USED

Bondcrete sealer. Paints are Jo Sonja Artist Gouache in Pthalo Blue, Pthalo Green, Raw Umber, Black, White and Pale Gold; Matisse Antique White; Chromacryl Cool Yellow. Winsor & Newton Gold Size

ABOVE

Thread the cherub charms onto the gold cord, which will be used to decorate the rim of the lamp shade.

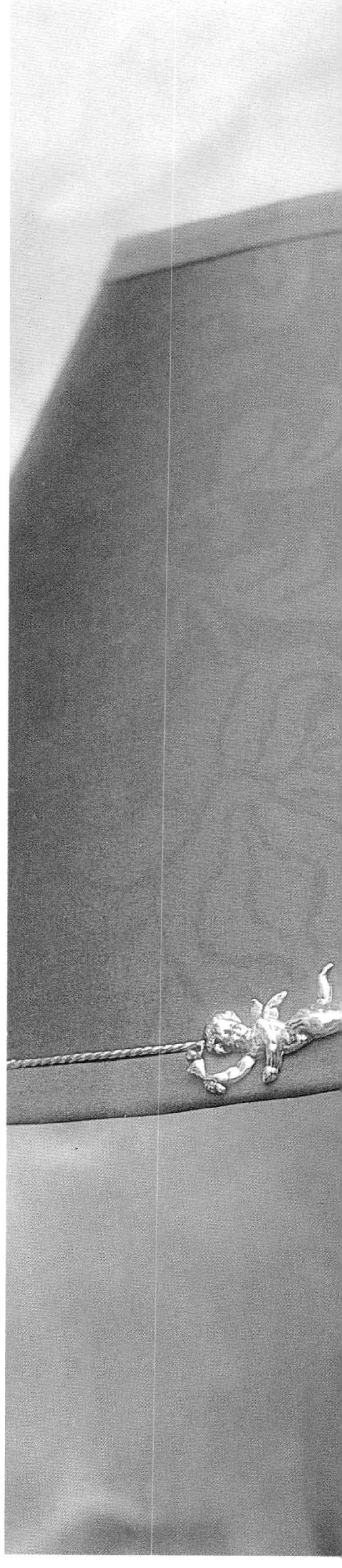

RIGHT

Verdigris and dappled gold lamp by Samantha Small

Dreams Divine

PROJECTS FOR THE BEDROOM

Stencilled frieze and picture mounts

Scherenschnitte picture

Embossed picture

Tea-stained print

Stencilled picture

Bed Linen

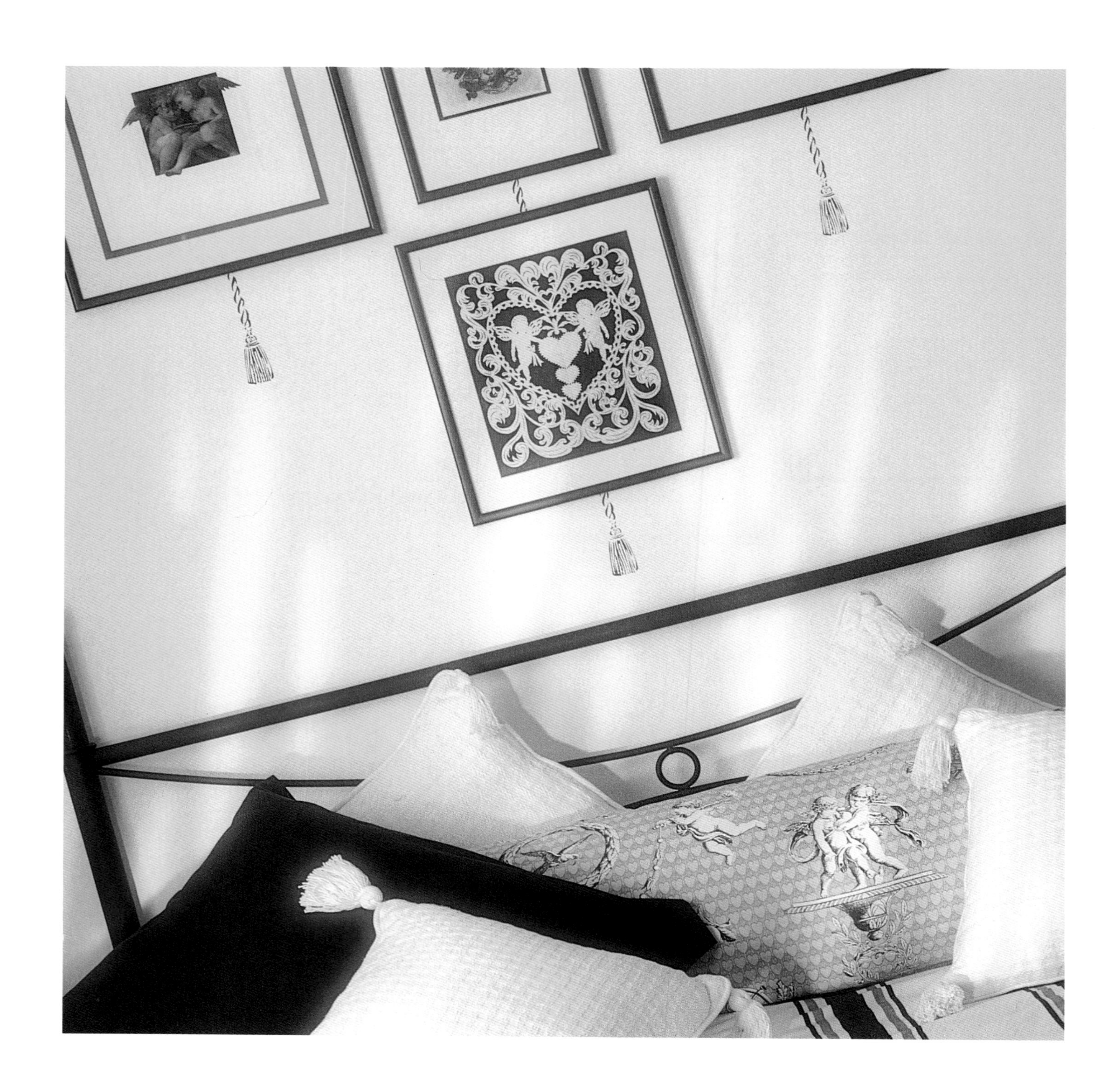

Dreams Divine

Stencilling is a marvellous way to add 'artwork' to any setting. In this elegant frieze of cherubs, cords and tassels, the hard work has already been done by our designer Elizabeth Nash; your job — the stencilling itself — is easy and lots of fun. The same stencil elements are used to create our picture mounts which 'hang' four very different cherub pictures, all of which are easy to make following our simple instructions. The bedroom is finished with bedlinen in smart black and ivory, with more cherubs waiting to lull you into a dreamy slumber.

LEFT

Sleeping in style: combine the cherubs you can make, such as those in our four pictures, with those you can buy — like this upholstery fabric — to create an elegant bedroom setting.

Stencilling

FRIEZE AND PICTURE MOUNTS

MATERIALS

Heavyweight drafting film
Scalpel
Cutting mat
5 large sheets of paper
Spray adhesive
No. 2 stencil brush
Black acrylic paint
Cloth
Masking tape
Ruler
Light pencil
Chalk line
Spirit level

WHAT WE USED

Stencils painted in FolkArt Acrylic Color in Licorice 938. Wall colour is Dulux Berkshire White.

TOP RIGHT

It is important to cut the stencils precisely, using a sharp-pointed scalpel, or they will be difficult to work with.

FAR RIGHT

Frieze and picture mounts designed by Elizabeth Nash

The stencil designs have been reproduced at the size we used them on pages 32–35. If you would like them smaller or larger, you can reduce or enlarge them on a photocopier.

1 There are seven elements to this design: two cherubs, a swag, a tassel, a bow, a straight piece of cord and a knot. Cut a piece of drafting film for each element, allowing plenty of space around each design — 8 cm gives you plenty of room to apply the stencil paint without fear of accidentally painting the wall! (If some pieces of film are a little small, you can add masking tape to the edges when stencilling.)

2 Trace each design onto the film.

3 Tape the film to the cutting mat. Using the scalpel, carefully cut out each stencil. These designs are quite fine and detailed, so allow yourself plenty of time. It is important to cut the stencils precisely, or they will be difficult to work with. If you are new to cutting stencils, you may like to practise first with some scrap film.

4 Onto each stencil, rule the guide line marked on the pattern, extending the line right to the edge of the piece of film.

continued on page 30

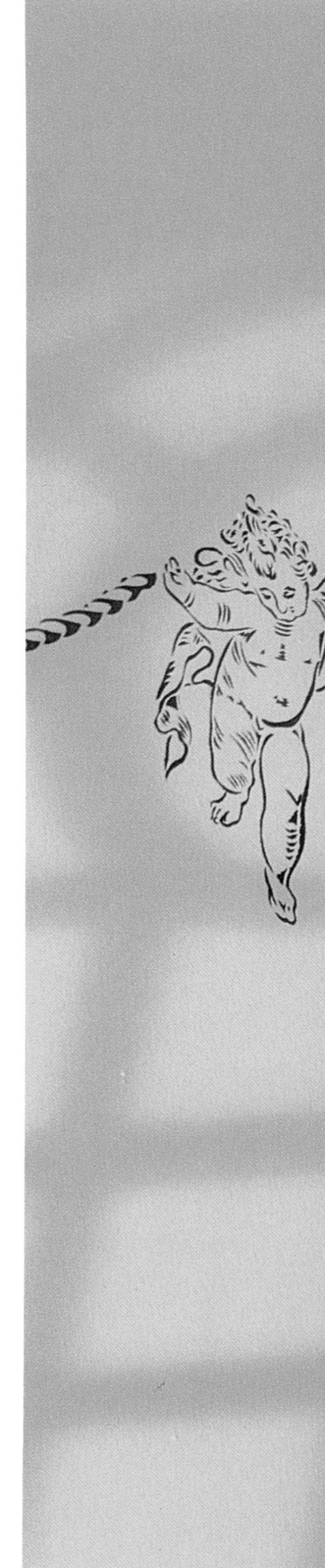

RIGHT
Apply stencil paint with a dabbing motion, working on small sections at a time.

5 Tape together three large sheets of paper for your masterprint. This will help you to plan where the stencil will go on the wall. Rule a straight line along the full length of the paper, then mark the centre line also.

6 Apply a light coat of spray adhesive to the back of your bow stencil. Place it so that its guide lines meet the two guide lines ruled on your paper, then press down firmly so that there is no space between the stencil and the paper.

7 Stencil the bow onto the paper. To stencil, pick up a small amount of paint with your stencilling brush, lay off excess paint onto the cloth, then dab paint all over the stencil. Work on a small section at a time, ensuring you have got paint into all the corners of the stencil. It is important not to get paint under the stencil, or the effect will be smudged. The masterprint is a good place to practise if you are new to stencilling.

8 Add two tassels underneath the bow. The first tassel uses the full tassel stencil only. For the second (longer) tassel, stencil the first three twists of cord at the top of the tassel stencil, then the tassel stencil in full. Always wait for the paint to dry before removing a stencil and going on to the next section. Artist's acrylics are especially designed to be very fast drying.

9 Stencil a swag on either side of the bow, and one of each cherub at the ends of the swags. Then add two further swags, and two more bows and their tassels.

LEFT
Remove stencils with great care to avoid both smudging the paint and tearing the stencil. With the cherubs and tassel stencils especially, where the loose pieces of film run in more than one direction, it is best to gently lift the stencil on two sides and slowly pull it away from the wall.

10 Use the masterprint to gauge the best position of the frieze on your wall. You may like to centre the frieze over a focal point, or you may like to simply start from a corner. The masterprint will show you which parts of the stencil will appear where.

11 Once you have decided where you want the frieze to appear, you need to mark the horizontal guide line. To do this, first make faint pencil marks where the guide line on your masterprint meets the wall, then use a chalk line to mark the guide line onto the wall. A chalk line (available from hardware stores) is easily removed after stencilling. Use the spirit level to ensure that the line is straight before marking it. Continue the line right around the room.

12 Starting at a point determined by your masterprint, stencil a bow and tassels as you did on the paper, then continue the design around the room. Renew spray adhesive occasionally.

13 Using two remaining sheets of paper, make up a masterprint for the picture mounts. These use the straight and knotted cord stencils in addition to the stencils used for the frieze.

14 Stencil the picture mounts onto the wall. The straight cords can be any length you like — simply re-use the straight cord stencil until you have the required length, then add the tassel.

continued on page 32

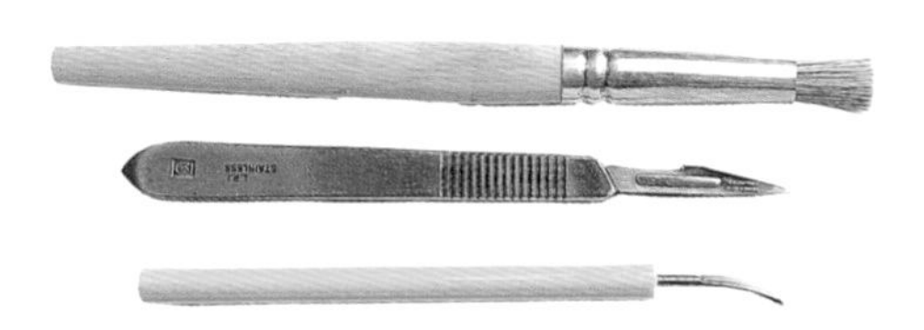

CORNERS

When you reach a corner, you need to leave space for the stencil element that will go around the corner, and then continue on the next wall.

• Carefully measure how much space the stencil element needs between the elements on either side. For example, in our corner shown on page 29, it is the bow that goes around the corner. The space the bow requires is not the width of the whole bow but the space from the tip of one tail (below the knot) to the next — this is where the two swag stencils join it.

• Mark the required space, starting at the stencil you have just finished, and mark the point where the first stencil after the corner should start. Begin work again at this point.

• When all other stencilling is finished (including the picture mounts), take the stencil required for each corner and cut it carefully along the line where the corner falls: it will be stencilled onto the wall in two parts. Take one part and place it in the corner, then tape over the edge and onto the other wall so that you do not paint any areas you don't mean to! Allow to dry, then repeat with the other piece.

You might also like to experiment with variations, using the same stencil elements. For example, you could use cherubs in the picture mounts, make the picture mounting area wider or narrower, 'hang' pictures direct from the cord in the frieze — the elements are here for you to use any way you like.

Of course, the stencils can be used for any number of other projects: matching bed linen, cushions, or the framed picture we have included — see our instructions on pages 46–47.

guide line for
left-side knot
guide line for
right-side knot

Scherenschnitte

SCHERENSCHNITTE PICTURE

MATERIALS

Parchment
(minimum 24 x 27 cm)
Scalpel
Cutting mat
Small sharp-pointed scissors
Grey transfer paper or light box
HB pencil
Pin

TOP RIGHT
Fold parchment in half and trace design onto right half.

FAR RIGHT
Scherenschnitte picture by Sandra Levy

1 Fold and crease parchment in half lengthways, then open out.

2 Using either the transfer paper or the light box, trace the pattern on page 39 onto the right half of the parchment.

3 Refold the paper along the crease line and start cutting out the design at the centre. Scissors can be used on the larger and outside areas, while the scalpel is better for small areas and the slits (the cherubs' facial features, hair, legs and bows around their waists).

4 Open out the design and place it face down on a piece of polystyrene or similar. Make pin pricks around the three central hearts and on wings, as indicated.

5 Place your scherenschnitte between two heavy books to flatten, then have it mounted on black card and framed.

LEFT

Scherenschnitte picture pattern

FAR LEFT

Scherenschnitte is the European craft of papercutting. The effect is very complex, but the technique is actually quite easy – with a bit of practice!

Embossing

EMBOSSED PICTURE

MATERIALS

Greeting card
Craft knife
Scalpel with No. 11 blade
Cutting mat
Watercolour paper
Embossing tool
Thick cardboard
Pencil
Ruler
Masking tape

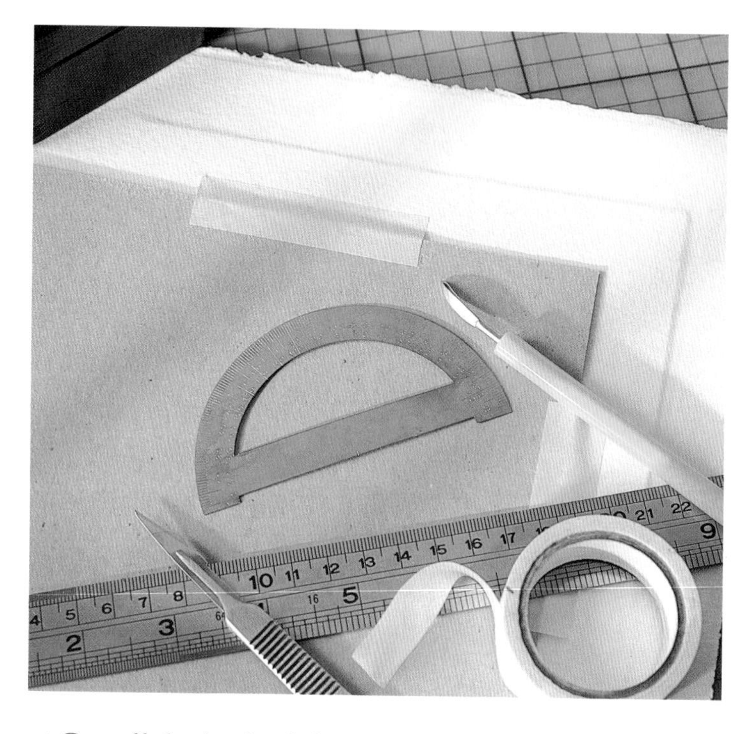

ABOVE RIGHT
With the embossing tool, work around the edges of the cardboard square.

FAR RIGHT
Embossed picture using a cherub greeting card

1 Cut off the back of the card. Cut lines around the pieces of the card which you want to overlap the mount (in our case the wings and one foot). Do not cut out the shape, rather leave the card its original size, with only the lines cut through.

2 Cut paper to desired size (in this case 27 cm square). From the lines cut through your card, you can determine the size of the centre cut-out (in this case 11 cm square). Cut this square from the centre of your paper.

3 Cut a piece of thick cardboard 1.5 cm larger than your centre cut-out (14 cm square). Very lightly tape this to the front of the paper, centring it over the cut-out, then turn your paper face down on the cutting mat. With the embossing tool, work around the edges of the cardboard, pressing gently at first and then more firmly (not too firmly!). Pay particular attention to the corners, then work embossing tool in small round motions to even out embossed line. Carefully remove the masking tape and cardboard.

4 Cut another square of cardboard 1 cm larger all round (16 cm square). Tape this to the bottom of the paper, then place the paper face up on the mat. Use the embossing tool to work around the edges of this second square, thus forming the outer edge of the square that surrounds the card. Work in small round motions to complete the embossed square. Carefully remove the masking tape and cardboard.

5 Cut a third piece of cardboard 4 cm larger all round (24 cm square). Tape this to the front of the paper, turn the paper face down on the mat and emboss a line around the edge. Carefully remove the masking tape and cardboard.

6 Place the card behind the paper and very gently ease the cut sections of the card over the paper. Tape the card in place at the back of the paper, taping at the corners only.

7 Have the image mounted and framed.

Print technique

TEA-STAINED PRINT

MATERIALS

Photocopies of selected artwork
Tea
10 mm brush
Masking tape
Scissors

WHAT WE USED

The image we used is Angel with Trumpet, a 16th century drawing by Luca Canbraso. It is in the Robert Lehman Collection (1975) in the Metropolitan Museum of Art.

TOP RIGHT
Paint strong tea over the photocopy, using long vertical strokes.

FAR RIGHT
Tea-stained 'print'.

1 Find an image you like (free from copyright restrictions) and enlarge or reduce it on a photocopier until it is the size you want. Take several copies so that you have a few to practise with.

2 Make up a small quantity of very strong tea, and paint it over the images in long vertical strokes.

3 Allow the images to dry flat, then choose the one whose 'stained' effect you like most.

4 Have the image mounted and framed.

This project is a variation on an old decorating trick called 'the printroom technique'. In that technique, the images are 'framed' by copies of elaborate borders and, once stained, the two are applied together direct to the wall, then finished with a low-sheen sealer. The print-room technique would be very effective with our stencilled picture mounts.

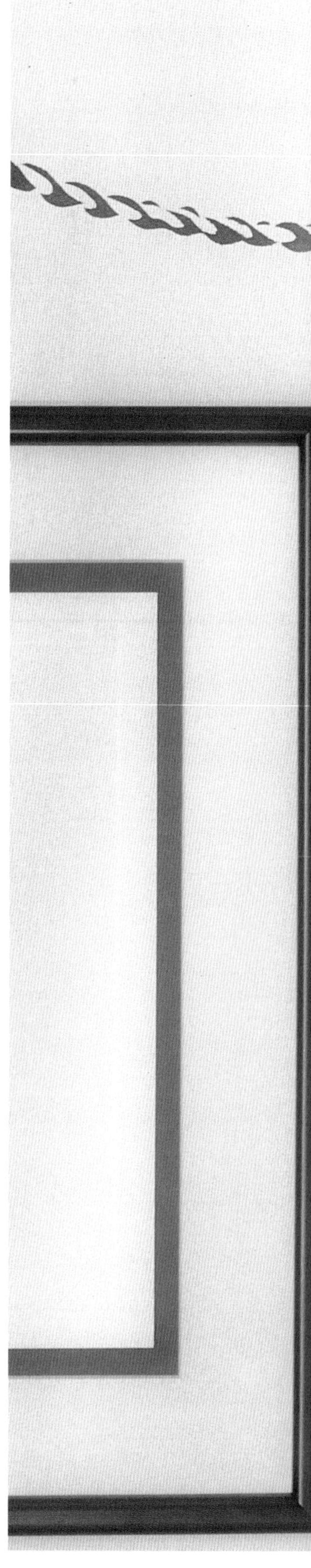

Stencilling

STENCILLED PICTURE

MATERIALS

Etching or watercolour paper
Ruler
Stencil as prepared for frieze
Stencil paint crayon
Stencilling brush
Spray adhesive

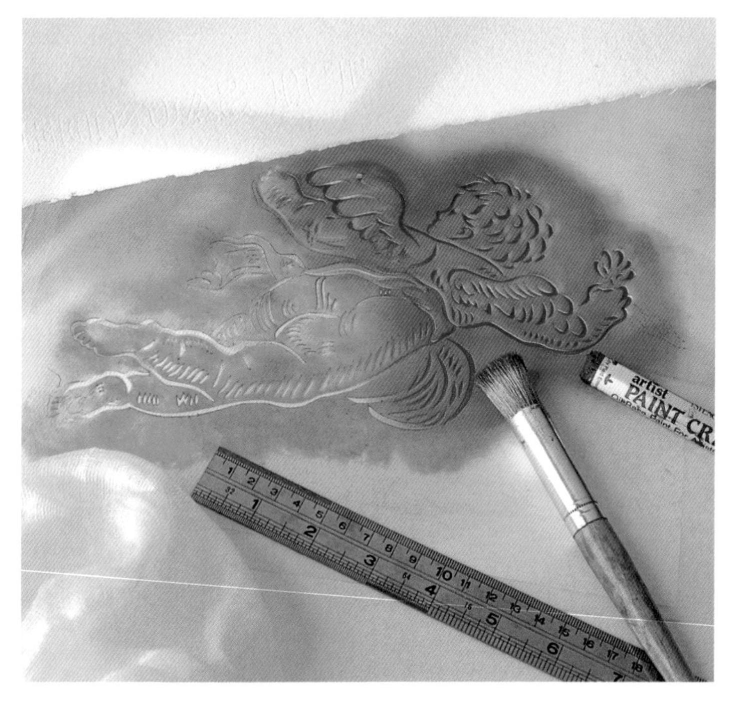

WHAT WE USED

Plaid's Artist Paint Crayon in 26535 Vintage Burgundy.

TOP RIGHT
Apply paint to the stencil film, then work it into the cut-out sections, building up the intensity of the colour until you are pleased with the effect.

FAR RIGHT
Stencilled picture using an element from the frieze

1 On the back of the paper, mark your desired finished size (in our case 21 x 29 cm). Place a ruler along each line at the back of the paper, and roughly tear the paper along the lines. Turn paper right side up.

2 Apply spray adhesive to the back of the stencil and centre it over the paper. Press down very carefully with fingers or a clean brush, ensuring that no gaps remain between the stencil and the paper.

3 Apply paint from the crayon onto the stencil, close to the cut sections. Working in small circular motions with your brush, pick up the deposited paint and work it into the cut-out sections. Repeat over full stencil, building up colour to the intensity you like.

4 Remove the stencil very carefully.

5 Have the image mounted and framed.

Of course, any of the stencil elements can be used to make a picture. You can use acrylic paint rather than crayon, but the crayon is very easy to use and gives a pleasing effect for smaller projects such as this.

BED LINEN

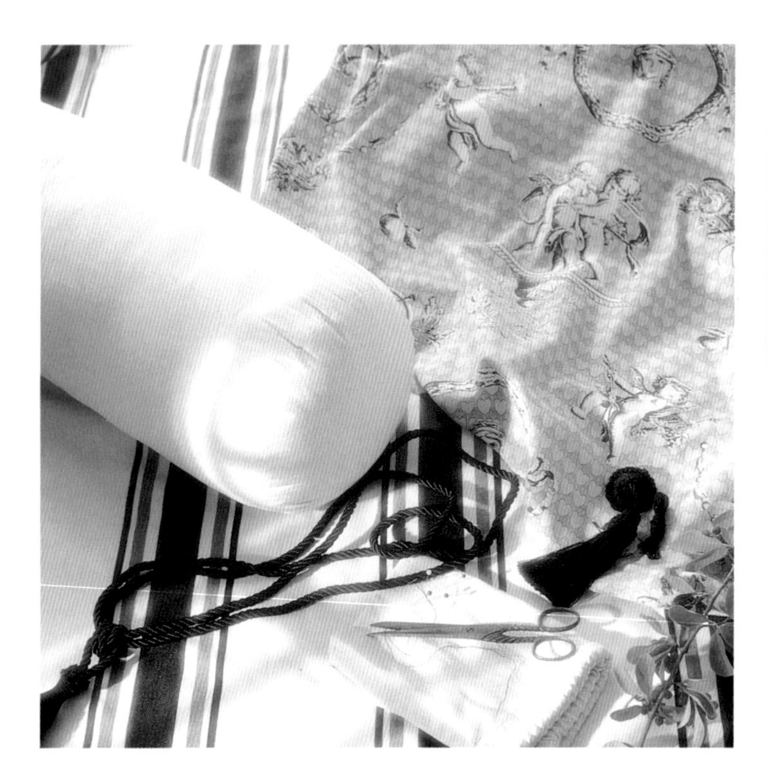

RIGHT
Smart, sophisticated bedlinen in black and ivory

With cherubs all around the walls and above the bed, you don't need to overindulge in cherubs on the bed too. Just one cherub fabric item is enough to continue the theme.

Here we have covered a bolster with a cherub print in black and ivory, then mixed this with a strong stripe from the same range, plus other cushions and pillow cases which pick up the ivory while adding textural interest.

It's easiest to buy the bolster insert ready-made, then make a simple cover.

1 Cut fabric to fit, plus seam allowances, and cut two rounds for the ends.

2 Make a long tube, fit one end, insert the bolster and then stitch in the other end.

3 Add black cord and a bolster tassel.

Keepsakes from Cupid

PROJECTS FOR
SPECIAL OCCASIONS
AND SPECIAL PEOPLE

Decoupage and folk art keepsake box

Gold charms on slippers

Cherubic bookmarks

Love-letters holder and other paper-covered items

Scented theorem pillow

Keepsakes from Cupid

Making and receiving beautiful gifts feature strongly among life's sweet pleasures. Here we present a range of special projects which you might make for yourself or for one of your favourite people. Either way, you are sure to enjoy making them and perhaps learning a new craft in the process. This chapter includes a pretty, embellished version of the traditional craft of decoupage, a European technique of stencilling onto velvet, the art of making paper-covered items, and a few very simple ideas with cherub charms.

LEFT

Labours of love: making beautiful things is always fun, but has a special charm when Cupid is involved, as you will discover while making any of the romantic projects in this chapter. Here a golden Cupid guest towel from Penny Lang does only a half-hearted job of concealing a love letter!

KEEPSAKE BOX

MATERIALS

Colour photocopy of card
Box
Cling wrap
Small sea sponge
Cloth
Rubber glove
No. 2 sable brush
25 mm flat brush
Sealer
Artist's acrylics in warm white, French blue, fawn, ochre, pearl, teal and green
Tracing paper
Black and white graphite paper
Stylus or old ballpoint pen to trace design
Scandinavian oil
Soft cloth
Artist's oil paint in burnt umber
Polyurethane satin varnish
Sandpaper (e.g. No-Fil Adalox A219)
Masking tape

TOP RIGHT
Create your image using a colour photocopy coated with sealer, then position it on the box lid.

RIGHT
Keepsake box by Merope Mills

1 Stretch a piece of cling wrap over work surface, wetting corners so it will stick. Place colour copy face up. Wearing a rubber glove and using your finger, apply a thin layer of sealer over whole card. Work horizontally and go over the edges of the card onto the cling wrap so as not to build up sealer at the edges of the card. Carefully remove card from cling wrap and allow to dry.

2 Apply five more coats, alternating between horizontal and vertical application.

3 When dry, cut out size and shape to fit box. (In our case, we cut a square shape so that the edges of the copy are underneath the ribbon.) Soak in hot water for an hour.

4 Remove from water and place face down on table. Using your thumb, gently rub off the paper — the image will 'stick' to the coats of sealer. Rinse image under running water and place on a kitchen towel to dry, ensuring that it is lying perfectly flat. It may look cloudy but it will dry clear.

continued on page 55

SONJA'S
Class I

5 If you are using the same card, trace the design on page 56 onto tracing paper as is. If not, modify the ribbon size to fit around your chosen image. Mark the position of the image on your box lid, according to your design.

6 Apply sealer to the back and front of the image, then position on box lid. Working from the centre, gently press out to the edges, removing all bubbles and getting the image as smooth as possible. Gently wipe off excess sealer with a damp cloth. Allow to dry for 24 hours, then sandpaper edges until smooth.

LEFT
Cover the lid in a warm white wash, then sponge on a cloud effect, blending in the edges of the image.

7 Using the flat brush and watered down warm white paint, paint a 'wash' from the edges of the image to the edges of the lid.

8 Mix warm white and French blue to make a very pale blue. Wet the sponge and squeeze out excess water. Dip sponge into pale blue and dab around picture, then repeat with warm white to create a cloud effect. Some of the sponging will go over the edges of the image. Continue around rim of lid.

9 Using the flat brush and watered down pale blue, paint a wash over the base and inside of the box.

10 Place your tracing of the design on the lid and secure it with a piece of tape. Place black graphite paper underneath and trace the design onto the lid with the stylus or pen.

11 Mix three parts fawn to one part ochre and one part pearl, and paint ribbon using sable brush.

12 Mix equal parts of teal, fawn, green and pearl, and paint centre of ribbon in this colour.

13 Position design on lid again and transfer lines for highlights using white graphite paper. Paint in the highlights using watered-down warm white, blending with a clean brush where colours meet. Paint a very fine line in warm white around edges of ribbon.

continued on page 57

14 The edging around the green stripe is painted in an equal mix of teal and fawn. Flatten your sable brush in the paint, then paint a fine line for the top of the 'twist', push your brush down (at a slant) thus broadening the stroke, then pull brush up again and continue with a fine bottom line. Look at the photograph at left to see this technique, and practise it first if you need to.

15 When all painting is dry, dampen a clean cloth with Scandinavian oil and wipe all over the box and lid, including the image. Add a very small dot of burnt umber oil paint and wipe over the image with the cloth, blending it out to the edges of the lid. Allow to dry for 24 hours.

16 Using the flat brush, apply three coats of varnish.

ABOVE
Paint the two-colour ribbon with the sable brush, then add the twisted cord outline.

WHAT WE USED

Sealer is Jo Sonja All Purpose Sealer. Artist's acrylics are Jo Sonja Warm White, French Blue, Fawn, Red Earth, Smoked Pearl, Teal Green and Moss Green.

Using Gold Charms

BOOKMARKS AND SLIPPERS

These pretty antiqued gold charms have a myriad of uses. In our following chapter, Festive Cherubs, we used them to embellish gift wrap and cards, while in Heavenly Hosts we used them to ring a lampshade and painted plant pots.

Here we have simply used them to dress up a pair of purchased slippers, and combined them with ribbons and cords to create a variety of bookmarks. These make easy, inexpensive yet very individual gifts.

ABOVE

Apply charms to slippers using a strong craft glue. For the bookmarks, ribbon and cord can be tied around the cherubs' wrists, waists or ankles or threaded through the holes at the back.

RIGHT

Gold cherub charms transform a pair of slippers and inspire four original bookmarks

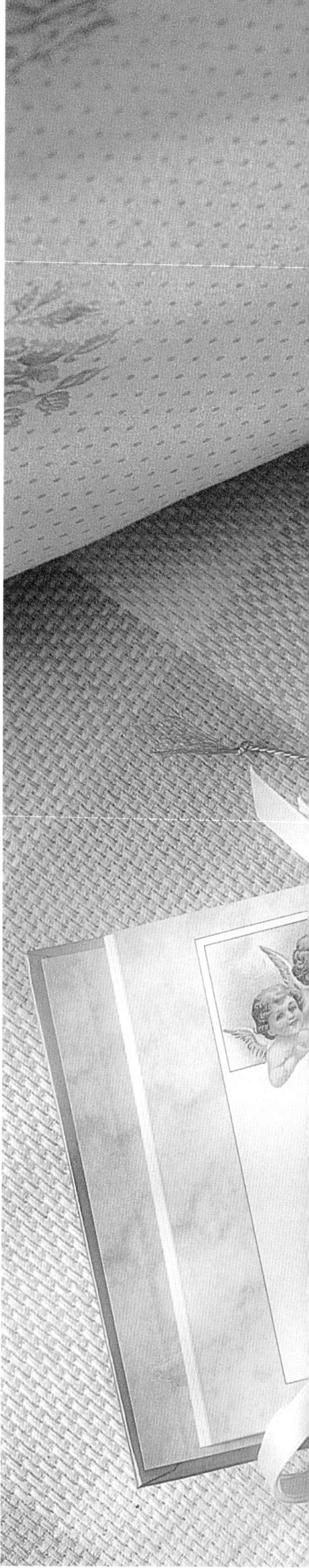

For He shall give His
angels charge over thee, to
thee in all thy ways.
They shall bear
up in their
hands, lest the
against a
THE
Little Book
OF

Paper-covering

LOVE LETTERS HOLDER

MATERIALS

Thick cardboard
PVA glue
Brush for glue
Self-adhesive bookcloth tape
Bone folder
Cutting mat
Steel rule
Craft knife
Scalpel with No. 11 blade
Wrapping paper
Toning plain paper for inside
60 cm ribbon
Sharp lead pencil

1 Cut two pieces of cardboard 20 x 27 cm, ensuring that corners are square. On both sides of both pieces, draw a line down one long side 4 cm in from the edge: this will form the spine. Then mark points 5.5 cm out from both corners opposite the spine and connect: these form the diagonal corner pieces.

2 Place the two boards side by side, with spines 0.75 cm apart. Apply bookcloth tape down each spine, lining up with your pencil mark and overlapping at top and bottom by 1.5 cm. The tape will overlap and thus connect the two boards. Turn the boards over and turn in the overlapping tape at top and bottom. Apply tape again to the inside of the spine, this time cutting it slightly short so that it does not overlap.

3 Cut a piece of bookcloth tape for each corner, leaving enough to fold back inside. Apply tape, lining up with pencil marks. Trim off any excess at the top of the piece of tape. Then, using the bone folder to ensure a neat finish, fold the tape around to the inside and trim it to line up with pencil mark before sticking down.

TOP RIGHT
From the wrapping paper, cut pieces for the front and back covers, centring your chosen pattern area.

FAR RIGHT
Love letters holder

continued on page 63

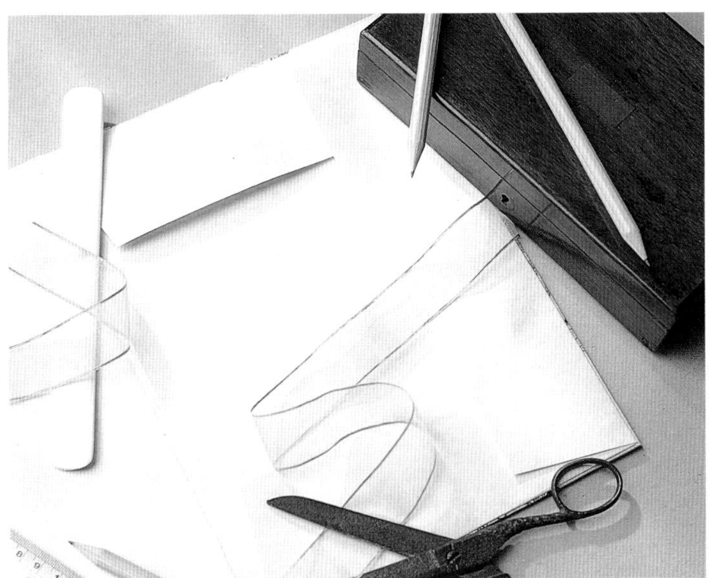

LEFT

Make the inside section from the toning paper. The right-hand side has three fold-ins

FAR LEFT

Other paper-covered items using purchased kits.

4 From the wrapping paper, cut two pieces 18 x 30 cm, centring your chosen pattern area. Place the front cover piece against the edge of the bookcloth tape, overlapping evenly on the other three sides. Carefully fold back and crease the two corners on the diagonal bookcloth tape lines. Cut these with the scalpel. Repeat for back cover. On the back of each piece lightly mark which is the front and which is the back cover.

5 Working quickly so the paper doesn't curl too much, brush glue onto the back of the wrapping paper and apply it to the cardboard. Gently remove air bubbles using the bone folder. Again using the bone folder, fold excess paper to the inside and glue it down.

6 Mark a line the width of your ribbon, centred 1.5 cm in from the opening edge on both front and back covers. Cut along these lines with the craft knife. Cut the ribbon in half and push a piece through each hole, gluing in place on the inside. Trim ends at an angle.

7 From the toning paper, cut out the inside section. On the left side it should be slightly smaller than the cover; on the right side it has three fold-ins 6.5 cm wide. Cut the ends of the fold-ins at an angle. Fold the inside section down the middle, then brush on glue and apply to the cover. Smooth out any bubbles using the bone folder.

8 Press holder under telephone books for several days, then fill it with your love letters!

Theorem

SCENTED THEOREM PILLOW

MATERIALS

Cotton velveteen in ecru, 35 cm square

5 sheets of 0.005 gauge Mylar, 40 cm square

Sharp-pointed craft knife

Cutting mat

Fine permanent marker

No. 2 stencil brushes (about 10 mm)

Artist's oil paints in burnt sienna, white, burnt umber, Prussian blue, crimson

Paint palette

Fine (No. 1) paintbrush

Mineral turpentine

Masking tape

Lavender or other scented sachet

Backing fabric, 35 cm square

1.5 m tassel trim

Cushion insert

TOP RIGHT
Using stencil 1 and colour A, stencil the cherub's body, arms and legs. Build up more colour at the edges for shading.

1 Number your sheets of plastic from 1 to 5. From the master pattern on pages 66–67, trace the appropriate stencil elements onto each sheet using the fine marker. Trace all the elements numbered 1 onto your sheet 1 etc. Carefully cut out the elements from each sheet.

2 Place the velvet on your work surface with the nap running down (so that it is smooth when you run your hand down it), and secure with masking tape. Position stencil 1 over the velvet and tape it to the work surface. Using a little of colour A (see key, page 67) on your stencilling brush, stencil the body and legs. Work from the outside edges to the centre, building up shading.

3 When dry, remove stencil 1 and position stencil 2, ensuring that the edge of the face lines up exactly with the top of the body you have already worked. Stencil the face with colour A, then move onto the other sections which are in different colours. Continue until you have completed all five stencils.

4 Use the paintbrush and burnt umber thinned with a little mineral turpentine to add facial features. Paint eyes in blue and add crimson cheeks.

5 Trim velveteen. Stitch trim to velveteen, finishing ends neatly. With right sides facing, stitch backing fabric to velveteen just outside line where trim is attached and leaving a gap at the bottom. Turn, place insert and scented sachet inside, then stitch gap closed.

FAR RIGHT
Scented theorem pillow by Sandra Levy

Trace outline of face only onto stencil sheet, not features. Use features as a guide when painting face.

Continue until you have completed all five stencils. You can create a more original, less uniform effect by varying a colour slightly — for example, by making the colour for the underside of the ribbon a little darker or by using different shades for the inner and outer parts of the wings.

Theorem is a very old decorative art, particularly popular in the late 1700s and early 1800s. It takes its name from the methodical method of using numbered stencils to create a unique piece of work with a large range of colours. Unlike some other forms of stencilling where a different stencil is used for each colour, in theorem the same stencil is sometimes used for several colours, as happens with this project. Also unlike other forms of stencilling, the sections are gently shaded rather than blanketed with solid colour. This helps to create the unique, hand-painted effect of a piece of theorem.

Stencil 1

Stencil 2

Stencil 3

Stencil 4

Stencil 5

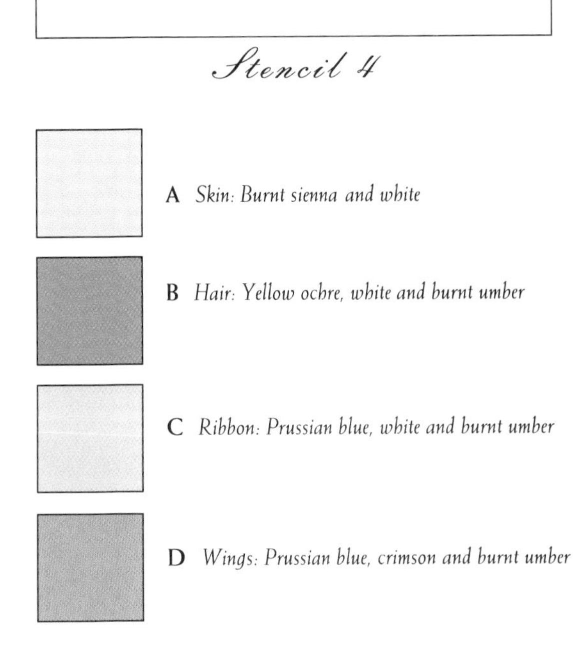

Festive Cherubs

PROJECTS FOR CHRISTMAS

Gift wrapping

Gilded oval box

Sponged gift boxes

Calligraphy cards and gift tags

Antiqued tree decorations

Christmas crackers

Noel
MERRY
CHRISTMAS
Isabella

Festive Cherubs

Christmas is an ideal time to introduce cherubs into your home. They lend themselves perfectly to all sorts of Christmas craft and decorating projects. We started by framing an enchanting greeting card as our version of 'the angel on the top of the Christmas tree', then continued with cherub tree decorations and cherubs scattered through all types of gift wrapping. A selection of cherubic Christmas cards are hung from the mantelpiece on gold curtain tiebacks. Even the Christmas crackers have more than a hint of our cherub theme. And who says Christmas always has to be green and red? Ours is at least as festive in pale blue, white and gold.

LEFT

Framed card for the tree: this project is as easy as can be. Simply choose your favourite card, then make up a frame, buy one to suit or have one made by a picture framer. Paint the frame gold if it's not already, then mount the card in it using foamcore (foam between two pieces of cardboard, about 5 mm thick, available from art suppliers). Cut the foamcore so that it fits very tightly into the frame. Add some gold rope (with thumb tacks) and a ribbon bow, and you have a delightful focal point for your tree.
Photographed at the home of Merope and Neville Mills.

Gift Wrapping

GIFT WRAPPING

At its worst, Christmas gift wrapping is the desperate, last-minute chore you wished you had started on much earlier. At best, it is a truly delightful way to spend an afternoon, either on your own or with a friend or two.

The first secret is to have all your gifts ready to wrap by your planned wrapping day, and the second is to have collected together an abundance of interesting materials. What you don't use now you can always use later.

By no means do all of the materials need to be expensive. Much of our wrapping here uses inexpensive tissue paper. Add to this a few more luxurious papers and a generous supply of ribbons. You can sometimes buy ribbons by the reel from wholesalers or discounters — ask some friends if they're interested in sharing a few reels with you.

RIGHT
Before you start, collect together an abundance of interesting materials.

continued on page 75

What you saved on inexpensive wrapping paper you might like to splash out on some finishing touches — the items that help make the difference between the ordinary and the gorgeous. These might include tassels, cords, stamps, seals, stickers, charms — don't look only in the gift wrap sections for inspiration, but try also stationery, craft, art supplies and haberdashery.

Finally there are the gift tags — but more about these on page 80.

Lay out all your materials when you have collected them. If you want to stay with a very specific colour theme, as we have, be ruthless in culling out anything which is not quite right, and putting it aside for another occasion. Then let your imagination set to work. Here are just a few possibilities.

- Use two papers together — either one tissue inside another or two papers on the one gift, divided by a ribbon.
- Tissue paper can look lovely when it's 'scrunched'.
- Use a stamp with gold ink to make your own luscious gift wrap from plain, inexpensive paper.
- Using more than one ribbon helps give a luxurious look to any gift.
- Use some tassels and cords as an alternative to ribbons.
- For those very special gifts, try gilding or sponging a gift box — see our full instructions on the following pages.

LEFT
Gift wrapping ideas with lots of impact

Gilding

GILDED OVAL BOX

MATERIALS

Small box
Cherub figure
Gold leaf (approx 5 sheets 10 x 10 cm)
Gold size
Craft glue
Cotton gloves
Small brush
Shellac/sealer
Varnish
Antiquing medium
Soft cloth
Gold cord

1 Stick figure to lid with craft glue, then seal box and figure with shellac or other sealer.

2 Paint size onto small section of box, and allow to cure for specified time (usually around 10 minutes). Then, wearing cotton gloves, gently press a sheet of gold leaf over sized section.

3 Repeat over whole box, then lid and figure. Press very gently over figure, or use a small, soft brush. If you miss a section, apply more size if necessary and press more gold leaf over size.

4 When the leaf and size are completely dry, very gently rub off any excess leaf, then apply varnish.

5 Carefully antique figure for extra definition by applying with a small brush and then wiping off immediately with a cloth.

6 Add gold cord around lid.

WHAT WE USED

Gold size from Winsor & Newton. Varnish is Feast Watson's Satinproof. Antiquing is FolkArt Waterbase Acrylic Antiquing in Blacksmith Black (815).

ABOVE
Gently press gold leaf over the sized sections.

RIGHT
Gilded oval box by Samantha Small

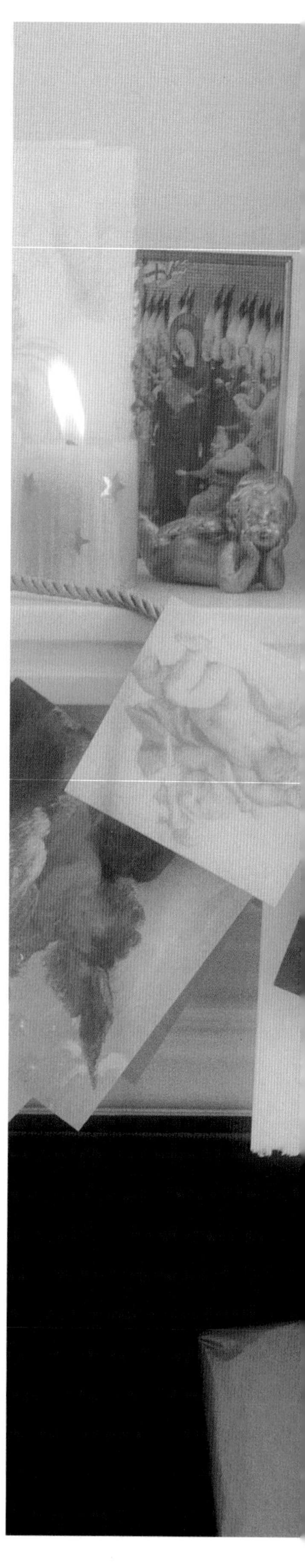

Isabella

Calligraphy

CARDS AND GIFT TAGS

MATERIALS

Selection of stiff papers or cardboards

Calligraphy pen and blue ink, or felt-tipped calligraphy pen

Pencil

Ruler

Embossing tool

Thick cardboard

Our alphabet for calligraphy appears on pages 84 and 85. If you are new to calligraphy, spend some time practising before you start on your cards.

1 First draw a baseline, then another line five pen widths (5pw) above it. The ascenders and descenders stretch three to four pen widths beyond these lines.

2 Holding your pen at the angle shown, repeat the eight exercises until you are happy with the result, then move on to practising the alphabet. Practise the minuscules (lower case letters), following the instructions given, then the majescules (upper case letters).

3 When you feel comfortable with your calligraphy, rule up your cards and set to work. As you gain confidence, you might like to add flourishes, dots or other decorations. Again, experiment with a variety of pens and techniques before you commit them to your cards.

You can further embellish your cards by embossing them with hearts or other shapes — see our instructions for embossing on page 40.

TOP RIGHT

As you gain confidence, you can add flourishes, dots and other decorations.

FAR RIGHT

Cards and gift tags by Dave Wood

Merry Christmas
Noel

Cancellarescha ∻ Chancery

DAVE WOOD FSSI 1994 ©

LEFT HANDED NIB

RIGHT HANDED NIB

45°

ANGLE OF PEN.

1 2 3 4 5 6 7 8

Good calligraphy should have: SHARPNESS in crisp fine lines
UNITY of slope, pen angle, form
FREEDOM.

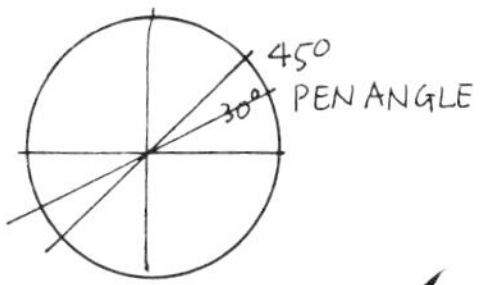

Majescules

DAVE WOOD FSSI 1994 ©

45° PEN ANGLE 30°

7 P.W. OR 8 P.W. NOT 9 P.W.

A B C D E F G I

START O 1 BELOW TOP LINE

H J K L M N O

P Q R R R S T U V

ABCDEEFGHIJKL
MNPOQRSTUVW
XYZ

W X Y Z & & &

OR 2 UP

5 P.W.

1 2 3 4 5 6 7 8 9 0 &

SHARPNESS · UNITY · FREEDOM ·

Antiquing

ANTIQUED TREE DCORATIONS

MATERIALS

Cherub figures
Gold spray paint
Antiquing medium
Soft cloth
Small brush
Ribbon
Gold thumb tacks
Hammer

When decorating your tree, hang the pearls (or similar decorations) first to give you your 'lines', then add the lights in between. If you have sufficient lights, don't just place them all on the tips of the branches but place some in close to the trunk — this adds plenty of 'dimension'. Our tree (two metres tall) takes 22 metres of pearls, 200 lights and around 50 decorations. If you will see all around your tree, you will need more decorations.

Making your own decorations certainly personalises your Christmas tree. These decorations are so simple to make that they are an ideal project to do with children.

1 Paint the figures back and front, making sure the paint covers all the details of the figures.

2 Antique them with an antiquing medium (available from craft suppliers). Antiquing takes the shininess off the gold paint and enhances the detail of the figures. It is applied with a brush and immediately wiped off with a soft cloth.

3 When the figures are dry, simply add a loop of ribbon. You may need a hammer to gently tap the thumb tacks into the figures.

TOP RIGHT
Paint the figures gold, then antique them to take off the shininess.

FAR RIGHT
Antiqued tree decorations

WHAT WE USED

Gold spray paint is FolkArt Color Matte Finish Paint (12136). Antiquing is FolkArt Waterbase Acrylic Antiquing in Blacksmith Black (815).

Papercraft

CHRISTMAS CRACKERS

MATERIALS

Papers
Cardboard tubes (one for each cracker plus two spare)
Snaps
Double-sided tape
String
Ribbons and other decorations
Gifts for inside

1 Cut papers the length of three tubes and wide enough to go around a tube plus 1 cm.

2 Place three tubes along the bottom of a piece of paper, then roll up tightly. Secure long edges of paper together using double-sided tape. Insert snap and gift.

3 Pull out first and third tube 3 cm each from ends, leaving centre tube in place. Carefully tie a piece of string between tubes to draw in paper gently and evenly. Remove string and tie both ends with ribbon. Remove first and third tubes.

4 Repeat for other crackers, then decorate.

We placed our crackers in a box lined with tissue paper and mesh (used in bookbinding). They make a lovely addition to other Christmas decorations around the home.

ABOVE
Roll the paper tightly around the tubes and secure with double-sided tape.

RIGHT
Christmas crackers decorated with cherubs, ribbons, cords and tassels

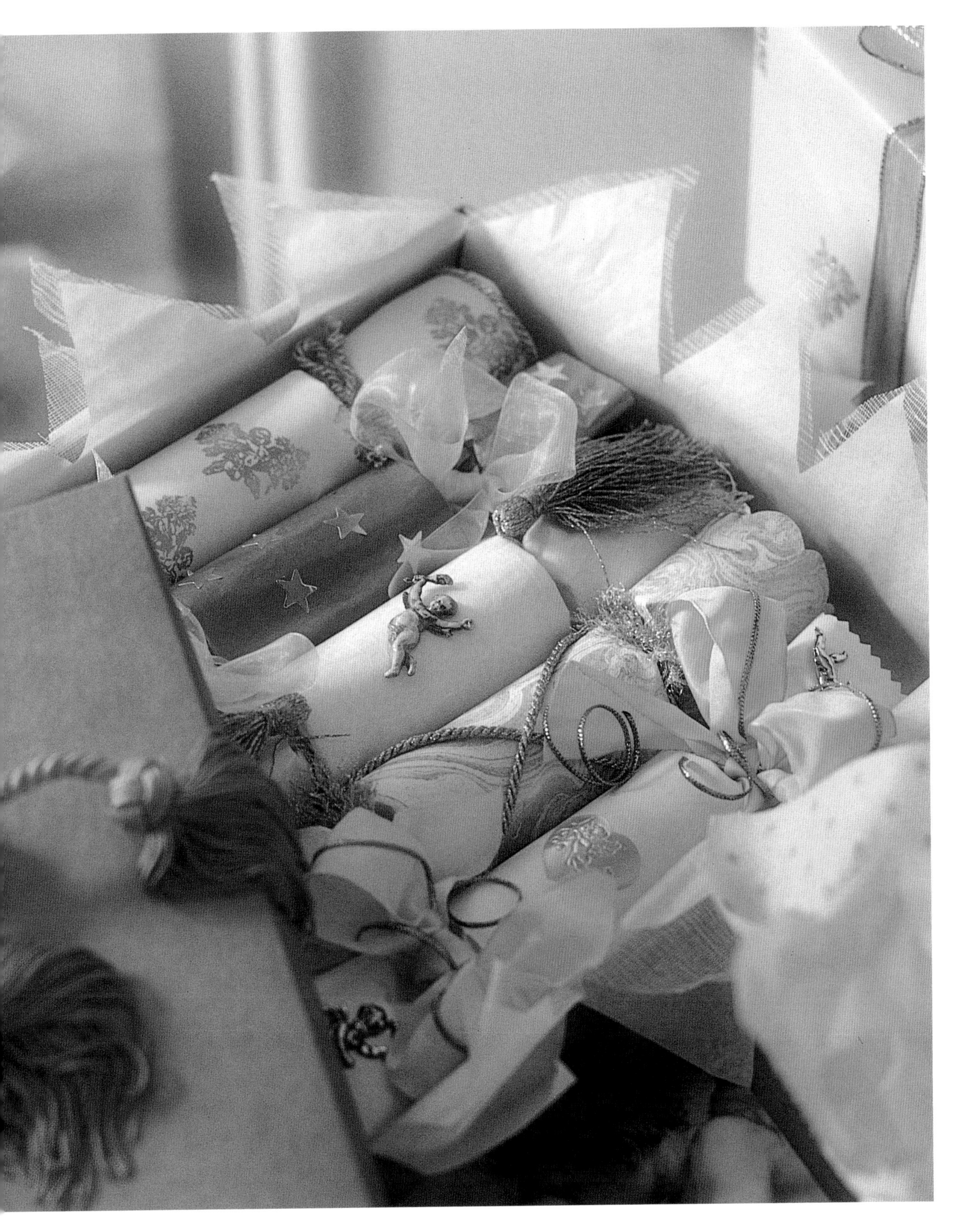

Craft Essentials

PRACTICALITIES

ABOUT THE DESIGNERS

21 22 23 24 25 26 27 28 29 30
NEED
30cm
9 STAINLESS STEEL 10 11 12in 12
MADE IN JAPAN
STAINLESS

Practicalities

There is a secret to the success of all of the stunning projects in this book — care and preparation. When you are starting your project, ensure that you have all of the materials you need to hand. It doesn't matter if you don't have the same brand we used, just make sure you have an equivalent product.

Check that your tools, such as brushes, embossing tools and scissors, are clean and don't have any residues adhering to them from previous projects. Check that your scissors and scalpel blades are sharp.

So many of the projects recommend a tack cloth or soft cloth for wiping over a project after sanding, so make sure that your cloth is clean and handy.

Careful preparation of the surfaces to be decorated will take a little time, but the extra effort is always worthwhile as you will have the 'feel' of the materials you are to use and so our detailed step-by-step instructions will simply fall into place.

When you are applying the paint on the stencils, or the glue to a dear little cherub or a rich gold cord, apply the paint or the glue gently and sparingly — you can always add a little more, but if there is too much there to start with it may be difficult to remove.

MATERIALS FOR PAINT CRAFTS

ACRYLIC UNDERCOAT is a gesso-like preparation which will provide a smooth surface for subsequent coats of paint.

ANTIQUING MEDIUMS are available ready-mixed or may be prepared with paint and maybe, varnish. They may be used to give a 'muddy' effect or to age the new look of a recently-painted project.

BASECOAT is a thinned paint and is available in water and oil-based forms. Some basecoats contain a sealer and either one or two coats are usually required.

BRUSHES are vital to most of the projects in this book. Always purchase the best brushes you can afford as cheap brushes are likely to shed their bristles at the wrong time, such as when the last coat of varnish or paint is being applied. Keep your brushes carefully — never on their bristles — and always make sure they are clean before you put them away. If you are going to do a lot of varnishing, for example, it may be an idea to keep a special brush only for varnishing. There are many, many types of brushes available: round and flat brushes with natural or synthetic bristles for folk art, stencil brushes, stippling brushes. The instructions for each project will tell you what size and type of brush you will need.

CUTTING MATS are available from craft and hardware stores. Use a cutting mat underneath stencil film when you are cutting out your stencil design, or underneath the paper when you are cutting scherenschnitte designs. The mat is self-healing and will not be cut by the stencil knife or scalpel and may be used many, many times.

DRAFTING FILM is available from specialist art suppliers. If it is to be used for cutting a stencil, use only a heavyweight film. See Mylar film.

FIXATIVE SPRAY may be used to seal one level of paint before proceeding to the next. The lower coat of paint cannot be disturbed by any problems which may result in subsequent layers.

GLUES are available in all types. We usually use a craft glue for the projects in the book. It is important to use a glue which dries clear and craft glues or PVA glues will work well for all our projects.

GOLD LEAF is very thin sheets of gold available from specialist art suppliers. It may be attached to a wax paper or sandwiched between thin sheets of paper. It is very light and very fragile. We recommend you handle it very gently while wearing clean cotton gloves.

GOLD SIZE is painted onto the surface onto which the gold leaf is about to be applied. It must cure for a short while (the time will be specified on the product) before the gold leaf is gently placed into position.

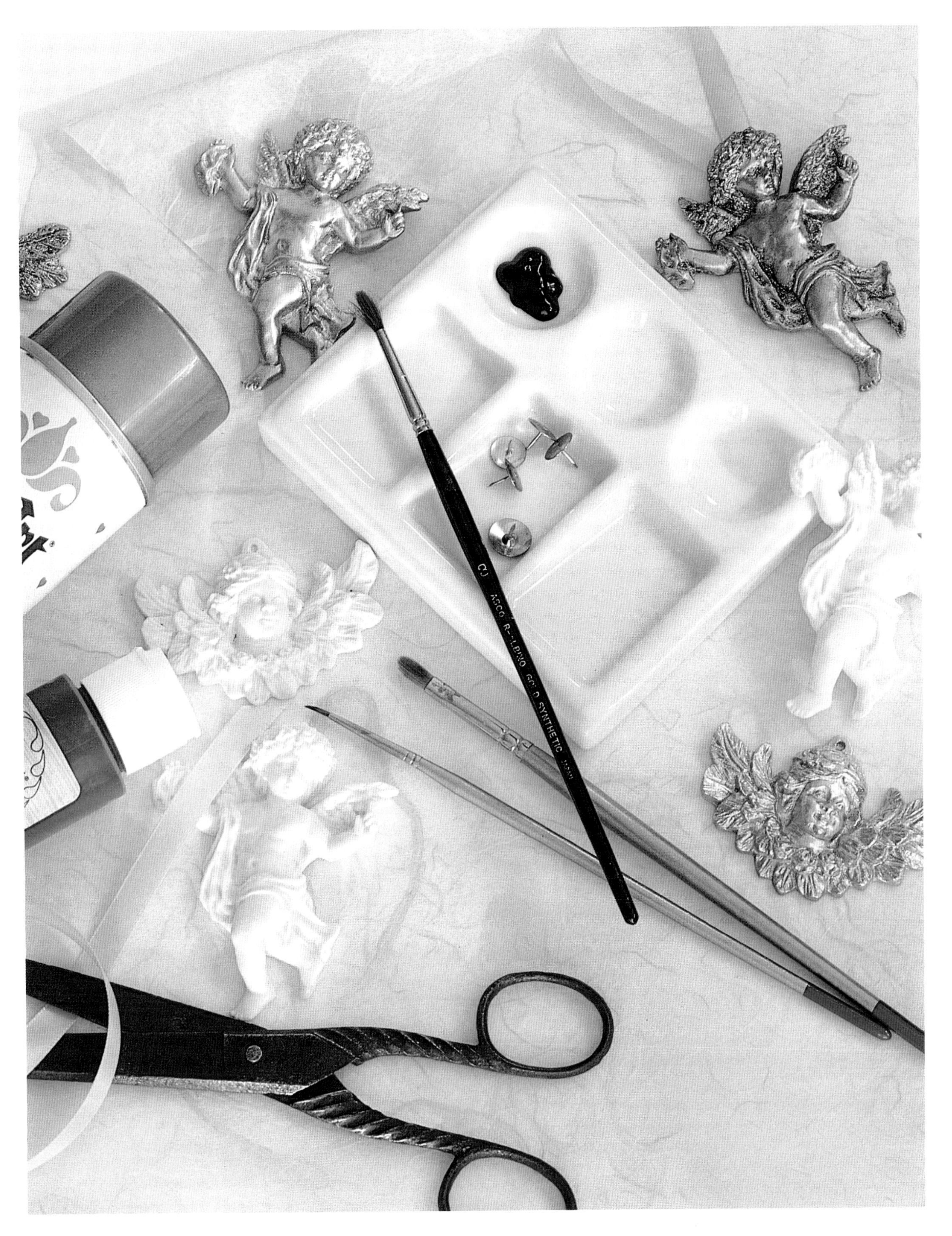
CJ
SYNTHETIC

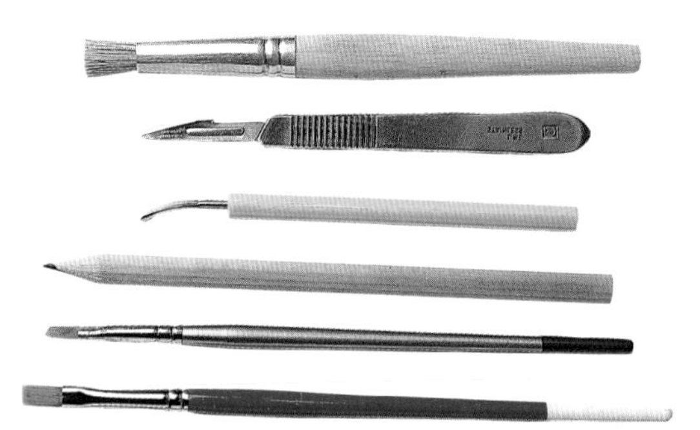

MASKING TAPE is readily available in many widths from hardware and craft stores and newsagents. The low tack masking tape is useful for projects where the tape must not damage the surface to which the tape must be applied temporarily. Masking tape is invaluable for painting straight lines.

MYLAR FILM is available in various sizes and is suitable for cutting stencils. Some Mylar stencil film has a roughened side to stop the stencil slipping while it is being used.

SCANDINAVIAN OIL is a finish for wooden items and is available from hardware stores.

SCISSORS are available is many, many types and different types are used for different purposes. In this book curved nail scissors are used for meticulous decoupage cutting, and sharp pointed scissors are used for the delicate detail of scherenschnitte. It is a good principle to keep paper scissors for cutting paper only and fabric scissors for fabric only. Using one pair of scissors for both materials is sure to blunt them very quickly.

SEA SPONGES will give a wonderful random 'clouded' effect. They are expensive, but with careful washing after each use will last a long time. Cellulose decorator sponges will give a similar effect but will need picking at with your fingers to soften the regular edges and to give an effect more like a sea sponge.

STENCIL PAINT CRAYONS are available in an oil-based crayon form in a range of colours. They are easy to use and the colours may be blended when the crayon is scribbled onto an uncut section of the Mylar film prior to loading the stencil brush.

TACK CLOTHS are used for wiping away dust from a project after sanding. They are available from specialist craft stores.

VARNISH is essential to seal painted finishes from moisture and wear and tear and to protect gold leaf from tarnishing. Often many coats of varnish are needed to build up a hard and durable finish. Light sanding with wet-and-dry sandpaper in between coats will give key to subsequent coats. It is usually a good idea not to apply varnish in wet or very humid weather as the varnish may turn cloudy (check the instructions on the product for advice). After a project has been coated with its many layers of varnish it will take some months for the maximum hardness of the varnish to develop so care during this time is recommended. The essential quality needed with varnish is patience.

MATERIALS FOR PAPER CRAFTS

BOOKCLOTH TAPE is a waterproof adhesive fabric tape used in bookbinding. It is available in various colours and the 50 mm width is recommended for the Love Letters Holder in this book.

BONE FOLDER: a tool used in book binding and other paper crafts to smooth down glued paper or other material onto another surface and to achieve neat folded edges.

CALLIGRAPHY PEN/felt tipped calligraphy pen: used to make the beautifully graceful lettering on cards, presents, pictures, etc. There are many different sizes of nibs and pens available from specialist art suppliers, stationers and good newsagents.

EMBOSSING TOOLS may be used for transferring designs in folk art as well as embossing. They have a rounded tip which is used for gently pushing the paper being embossed. The tools may have one tip or may be double ended with two different sized tips.

SPRAY ADHESIVE is available in aerosol form and is most useful as a temporary adhesive. Always use it in a well-ventilated space. After use invert the can, point it towards a sheet of newspaper and press the spray button on the can until no adhesive is sprayed from the can. This ensures that no adhesive remains in the spray mechanism of the can and means that all the contents of the spray adhesive can may be used.

TRANSFER PAPER is a non-greasy paper used for transferring designs to another surface. It is available in black, grey and white.

About the Designers

ALEXANDRA GRAY designed our embellished decoupage serving dish on page 12. The dish is a beautiful example of Alex's work, which takes the traditional craft of decoupage and adds a whole new dimension with the clever application of paint. Her skill as an artist in mixed media results from her extensive studies of art in many forms. Alex has exhibited extensively in Sydney and her work is now represented in collections in Australia and the United Kingdom.

SANDRA LEVY is a prolific craftsperson who has mastered a remarkable array of crafts, including some lesser known ones which she has used in creating two projects for this book. Sandra first learnt about the European craft of scherenschnitte (papercutting) from a magazine article and has gone on to develop both her skills and her knowledge in this field; she is now one of only two Australian members of the American Guild of Papercutters. Sandra created our scherenschnitte picture (page 36), which she assures us is easier than it looks! Another of her favourite crafts is theorem, the art of stencilling onto velvet, and from this she has designed our pillow on page 64. Sandra travels regularly to America to learn more about her many crafts, but when at home runs a number of popular classes.

MEROPE MILLS, who created our keepsake box on page 52, is well known in Australia for her mastery of decoupage and European folk painting (Bauernmalerei). Merope first learnt these skills in her native South Africa. When she moved to England she combined them with her background in teaching and began her first classes. Now, after 13 years in Australia, Merope's classes are in tremendous demand, covering a delightful range of projects. Merope also undertakes commissions and exhibits her work widely, and she has produced a number of instructive books including *Imaginative Brushwork* and the *Heirloom Project Books: Victorian Lace & Roses, Hollyhock Cottage* and *Heritage Album.*

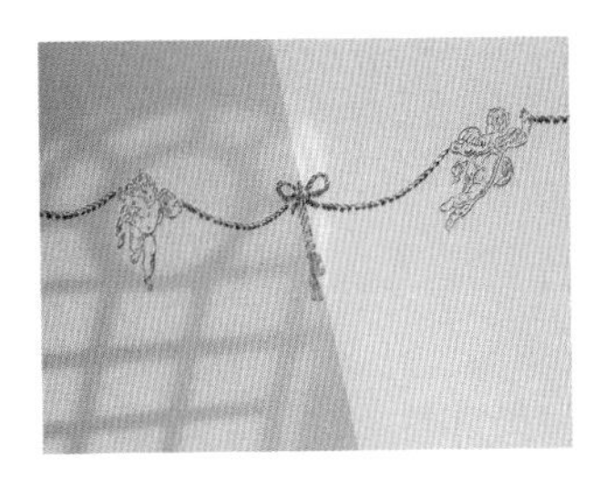

ELIZABETH NASH of Stencil Design in Melbourne created our wonderful stencilled frieze and picture mounts (page 28). Her ability to add unmistakable style and elegance to that bedroom is not so surprising — Elizabeth trained as an interior decorator in Melbourne, and worked and taught in that field for some ten years. Since then she has established the successful Stencil Design, a company which not only sells ready-made stencils and undertakes stencilling commissions but runs classes so that anyone can learn how to use stencils and other paint finishes to great effect.

Samantha Small is a creative young paint finish artist who in just a few years has progressed from teaching herself techniques from books such as this one to running her own paint finish company, after a stint with one of Sydney's leading residential paint finish firms. Samantha created a number of our projects — the gilded and sponged gift boxes in our Christmas chapter (pages 78 and 79), as well as the verdigris and dappled gold pots and lamp (pages 18 and 22) and the stippled statue (page 16) in our outdoor dining setting.

Dave Wood, who executed the beautiful lettering on our cards and gift tags (page 80) and on our placecards (page 10), is well known in the calligraphy field for his highly creative work over a number of years. He learned the basics of his craft in Manchester, England, where he was apprenticed as a poster writer while studying at Art School. He then worked as a graphic designer in New Zealand until coming to Australia seven years ago. Dave now runs classes in calligraphy and drawing, as well as exhibiting widely. He is a Fellow of the Society of Scribes and Illuminators and a Member of the New Zealand Society of Industrial Designers.

Louise Owens graduated from the University of Technology, Sydney (UTS) with a Bachelor of Design (Interior Design) with First Class Honours. Louise now runs Owens Interior Design, doing both residential and retail work as well as styling home and craft features for books and leading magazines. Louise is a member of the Design Institute of Australia and has lectured interior design students at UTS.

Kate Tully has a BA (Communication) from the NSW Institute of Technology. After several years on the staff of specialist magazines she formed Communicate — a writing and editing consultancy — in 1985. Kate has contributed many feature articles to decorating and crafts magazines, and is also the author of a number of books on these and other subjects.

Louise and Kate are sisters who both live in Sydney. They have worked together on a large number of craft and decorating books, and have also jointly developed and presented decorating training courses. As well as that, of course, for as long as they can remember they have collaborated — sometimes with other members of their family — on craft and decorating projects for their homes and their favourite people.

The publishers would like to thank the following individuals and organisations for their generous help during the production of this book:

A D Imports for plain tissue and embossed "Perla" papers (PO Box 145, South Yarra Vic 3141 Tel (03) 826 6004)

Aird Imports for Portal cards, pages 53 and 69 (Tel (08) 232 0788)

Artistic Renditions Studio for painted cherub charm and painted cherubs and brooches (258 The Parade, Norwood SA 5067 Tel (08) 332 8317)

Castle Trimmings for bolster tassels (696 Old South Head Road, Rose Bay North NSW 2030 Tel (02) 371 0066)

Catherine's Cottage for fabric covered box and wicker table (756 Pacific Highway, Gordon NSW 2072 Tel (02) 418 1909)

Chas Clarkson for Christmas baubles (465 Kent Street, Sydney NSW 2000 Tel (02) 267 1571)

Creative Craft Kits by Helen Norton for gold cherub charms and kits for paper covered items (PO Box 111, Gordon NSW 2072 Tel (02) 983 9972)

Designer Trim for gold cords, tassels, ribbons and tassel trim (473 Elizabeth Street, Surry Hills NSW 2010 Tel (02) 310 1777)

DMC -Myart for gold paint, Folk Art and Plaid paints

Freedom Furniture for Kensington lamp base

Gallery Collection for gift wrap (PO Box 51, Port Melbourne Vic 3207 Tel (03) 645 1166)

G L Distributors for Christmas cracker snaps (PO Box 222, Smithfield NSW 2164 Tel (02) 606 9377)

Harvey Norman Arncliffe iron bed

House of Craft for velveteen (Tel (02) 440 0115)

Jaan for boxes and resin cherub figures (16 Roylston Street, Paddington NSW 2021 Tel (02) 331 4940)

J B Heath for gold leaf (Dutch Gold Metal) Tel (03) 807 8578

Julia Walton Designs for ceramic sitting cherub (22 Maranoa Street, Wyoming NSW 2250 Tel (043) 29 1588)

Penny Lang for screen-printed cards, black cherub box, screen-printed towel and T-shirts (10 Phillip Street, Neutral Bay NSW 2089 Tel (02) 908 4253)

Laura Ashley for lamp shade

Linen and Lace of Balmain for tassels, cords, pot pourri bags, linen, tin bucket and floor mat (213 Darling Street, Balmain NSW 2041 Tel (02) 810 0719)

Lisa Milasas for all fresh flowers (300 Sylvania Road, Gymea NSW 2227 Tel 018 166 087)

Mon Imports for marbled and recycled papers (PO Box 310, East Kew Vic 3102 Tel (03) 428 0242)

No Chintz for bolster insert (574 Crown Street, Surry Hills NSW 2010 Tel (02) 318 2080)

Offray Ribbons for wired and satin ribbons

Optimism for Santoro Graphics paper, page 61 (47 King Street, Newtown NSW 2042 Tel (02) 519 9932)

The Parterre Garden for plants and gold pears and for providing such a delightful setting for photography (33 Ocean Street, Woollahra NSW 2025 Tel (02) 363 5874)

St James Furnishings for cherub and striped fabrics (100 Harris Street, Pyrmont NSW 2009 Tel (02) 660 1544)

Scarpa Imports for Woodmansterne cards, pages 69 and 70 (Tel (03) 500 9867)

Stamp World for stamps and gold stamp pad (145 Beattie Street, Balmain NSW 2041 Tel (02) 818 3111)

Star Cards for stationery (5 Stuart Street, Armadale Vic 3143 Tel (03) 500 0080)

Stitches Soft Furnishings for making the pillow (103 Regent Street, Chippendale NSW 2008 Tel (02) 698 4399)

Sydney Framing Centre for all framing in Dreams Divine (Westfield Chatswood, 1 Anderson Street, Chatswood NSW 2067 Tel (02) 412 4433)

Via Rustica for bedside table and pots (3 Lord Street, Roseville NSW 2069 Tel (02) 416 1113)

Will's Quills for book cloth tape and bone folder (164 Victoria Avenue, Chatswood NSW 2067 Tel (02) 411 2627)

The Wren Press for place cards (316 Rockeby Road, Subiaco WA 6008 Tel (09) 388 2188)

Published by Grange Books
An Imprint of Grange Books PLC
The Grange
Grange Yard
London SE1 3AG

Produced by Hodder Headline Australia Pty Limited,
(A member of the Hodder Headline Group)
10-16 South Street, Rydalmere NSW 2116, Australia

This edition published in 1995

ISBN 1 85627 674 0

Concept - Joanne Morris
Design - Clare Forte
Craft consultant - Alsion Snepp

Printed in Australia by Mc Pherson's Printing Group, Melbourne